The Legend of the Twilight Owls

A Book of Poetry for the
Searching and the Perplexed

Mayer Wisotsky

Also by Mayer Wisotsky:

The Woodcarver, 1981

Meriel Wisotsky, Mayer's wife, painted all the owls in the book. She works with several media, including her unusual paintings of animals on tin can lids. An artist with a Fine Arts degree from California College of Arts and Crafts, she can be reached at *merielwisotsky@gmail.com*.

The Legend of the Twilight Owls

A Book of Poetry for the Searching and the Perplexed

Mayer Wisotsky

Copyright © 2021 by Mayer Wisotsky

All Rights Reserved. No part of this book may be reproduced, stored in a retrieval system, or transmitted in any form or by any means, electronic, mechanical, photocopying, recording, or otherwise without the prior written permission of Mayer Wisotsky or his assigns.

ISBN: 978-1-7351438-5-9
Library of Congress Control Number: 2021910756

Original artwork by Meriel Wisotsky

Designed by Linda A. Hamilton
Published by Stories to Last Publishing
Oakland, CA
www.StoriestoLast.com

Stories to Last

Dedication

I dedicate this book to my wonderful partner in life,
My Wife Meriel
She has been my editor and chief critic throughout
the whole process
of writing and assembling
all of the parts necessary
to produce this book.

Table of Contents

The Legend of the Twilight Owls	9
Introduction	10
Who Am I?	13
Who Are They?	53
Love	73
Loneliness	91
Change	105
Death	125
Paradox	145
About the Poet	176
Poetry as a Medium for Creative Expression	178

The Legend of the
TWILIGHT OWLS

THE WISDOM OF THE OWLS is legendary. Since Ancient Greece, when an owl sat on Athena's blind side so she could see the whole truth, the owl has been a symbol of higher wisdom.

Owls were given the ability to understand the significance of all human experience. This made them very wise indeed. Even in the twilight, they persist in giving their opinion (based on their observations) on every subject in the world.

In this book they pass along the essence of their wisdom in the form of poetry. Each poem exposes another morsel of truth and understanding of our wonderful universe.

Introduction

I ACQUIRED THE UNDERSTANDING of my world through the living of the bits and pieces of my life. It formed the understanding of my Universe.

My existence caused me to Question. My knowledge gave me Direction. And my experience produced Answers. Putting them all together gave me Wisdom. Wisdom only I can use—only I can understand.

The path I took stretches to Infinity, no end in sight, just little glimmers of hope along the way. But there is enough for me to make the road worth taking. The obstacles were formidable and seemed impossible to overcome, but their existence was key to the learning and eventual understanding of myself and my world.

Along my path, I wrote in verse and prose to leave a record of this journey, of My Life in My Universe. This collection expresses the wisdom gained in the Twilight of My Life.

I have divided my writings into seven categories:

1. Who am I?
2. Who are they?
3. Love and its virtues.
4. Loneliness and frustration.
5. Change and its consequences.
6. Death and its meaning.
7. The paradox of it all

These phases are arbitrary of course, but still provide a way to organize the information, the understanding and the wisdom that I have acquired. Nothing happens in a vacuum; everything is connected. But each poem or writing is individual in itself and explains that slice of my life.

If anything speaks to you from this book, take it, use it and answer it back. Tell it how you feel. Tell it what you think and maybe it can help you understand your life and help you find your wisdom.

WHO AM I?

Poems exploring the perception of self
Acceptance of self—rejection of self—
And the resurrection of self

MAYER WISOTSKY

The Deserts of My Soul

The desert sands burn my feet,
Yet I wander on.
The blazing heat dries moisture from my lips,
Yet I speak to the sun.
Pain is my companion,
Suffering becomes my end.
Yet I must explore the deserts of my soul.
I must know the part that pleasure
Cannot reach.
I must know the part that contentedness
Cannot teach.
The desert sands may burn my feet,
Yet I must wander to find the wonderment
I will meet.

April 6, 1978

THE LEGEND OF THE TWILIGHT OWLS

Where Is My Mountain?

Where is my burning desire?
That all-consuming passionate fire,
For that distant goal,
Dictating my every action?
That mountain peak where all is justified,
All serene?
I look in vain for who I am or was.
There are no answers,
Only more questions of why and who,
What I should or shouldn't do.
All paths are fine,
When there are no mountains to climb!
But there is an essence to my being,
A part of me that is apart,
Connecting me to the unity--
The oneness of my being,
The totality of what I have been,
With the infinity of what I can be,
Where the answers to my questions lie,
Where my journey begins.
Where the fog lifts,
And the base of the mountain appears.
I ascend upon the path
Leading into clouds.
Believing there is a peak,
I shall someday reach,
Where ecstasy will forever fill my soul.

Created July 14, 1998; updated August 24, 2017

MAYER WISOTSKY

The RIVER

To be Immortal is to be the River
Not just the Water
The shore belongs to the River,
But the shore confines and defines the River.
The water belongs to the River,
But the water determines if the River is high or low,
Fast or slow.
The things that live in the water belong to the River,
They give it color and vitality.
They depend on the River for their Being,
Yet the River depends on them for its changes and development.
Oh! To be the River--to be objective--unfeeling, but caring--wild, but responsible.
I am my boundaries, I am my contents, I am my changes,
From the beginning of my life to its end.
I run swiftly in the rough terrain of Life,
Lie silent in the broad plains of contentment,
Cut deeply in the highlands of ambition,
Meander widely in the lowlands of success.
I flood during violent emotions,
Run dry during bad times of remorse,
Flow bountifully in good times of inspiration.
For I am the River in all its totality
And soon I shall become the Sea.

August 1, 2004

The Nobler Man

Though I sit upon a chair,
Though I never comb my hair,
Though I think I know my end,
Still I doubt I know my fate.
I try to be the end of time.
I try, but still, my life remains,
No rhyme or reason to its path.
I walk with powers greater than myself,
Yet feel alone when they cause me discontent.
I cling to knowledge I do not possess,
A sight from the bottom looking up.
A lesser man might be filled with despair,
A vainer man might never care,
But the Nobler Man, of which I am one,
Will take the challenge, embrace the cause,
Climb the mountain, ignore the pain,
Find life worth living.
To happily sit upon a chair,
And joyfully never comb my hair.

January 5, 2014

MAYER WISOTSKY

Fragile

Our lives, like jigsaw puzzles, carefully pieced together over
Time,
Carefully examined for shape and color, meticulously put
Together so that all things would fit--
Without even knowing how the final picture would look.
These fragments of our being, which we call "I" and "Me,"
So fragile to the touch,
Breaking apart with the merest wave of God's hand,
The slightest puff of breath,
Then our lives fall to pieces again.
All the bits we knew so well become strange and scattered,
Then we go about the task
of building "Me" all over again.

July 7, 2014
Revised May 2, 2018

Furry Face

I wake each morning to a furry face,
A gentle paw upon my eyes,
A squeaky voice of dire intent:
"Get up, old man. It's time to eat!
The day is beginning, and my stomach aches!
It's time to eat! Get out of bed!"
I swat the paw and say,
"Go away; it's too early to eat, besides it's Saturday."
I protest, but to no avail,
The squeaky voice and paw persists.
My eyelids won't stay closed.
So I look at my cat,
Expecting to see his sorrowful furry face,
Begging for my assistance.
But like a magician making things disappear,
He changes his pitiful stance,
Looks at me instead with an air of great concern,
Saying,
"Good morning, dear friend, why are you up so early?"

August 11, 2014

MAYER WISOTSKY

Growing Old

Where is the joy I knew so well?
When I was just a child,
When I was just a boy?

Where is that thrill of discovery,
That filled my emptiness with satisfaction?
How happy I was to find a leaf, a bug, a butterfly,
Even a smooth rock made me sigh.
Loving the acceleration of running down a hill,
Of splashing in a puddle of rain,
Or feeling warm sand between my toes.
Where are those days when life was vital
And I was bold?

In the other room you say?
In heaps of scrapbooks tucked away?
That's where they linger now that I am old,
And soon even they will be gone.
But life does not flourish on bits of paper,
In pictures or celluloid tapes.
So all I was and all I did, I've tucked into my bones,
And I carry all those memories
As building blocks of my today.
Living my life more fully
As I bound along my way.

February 11, 2015

The Vegetarian

One day while looking for myself I posed a dreadful question,
"Who is in control of what you eat, you or your stomach?"
The question was immense; it challenged who was in control;
It threatened me to my very core. So I made a bold decision:
Tomorrow morning I would become a vegetarian
Because of how much both my stomach and I loved to eat meat.
In the morning as I awoke ready to eat no meat,
A whiff of heaven crossed my nose: the smell of bacon frying.
"Oh God," I cried in great despair, "This can't be happening to me!
Not now! I have just begun a test that will prove the power of me."
But the smell was strong and filled the room…
I sat upon the bed, trying to resist temptation's call.
Suddenly my mind whirred into motion and created a very
Powerful notion!
Could I possibly enjoy the smell without ever eating the bacon?
Could this single moment of pleasure be an eternity leading
Nowhere but to itself?
Could that moment be forever? Never leading to eating the bacon?
And could my life be made of many moments, just like this one?
Today I am a vegetarian who found out who was boss,
Who lives every moment as an eternity, where pleasure has no cost,
And nothing ventured is ever lost.

September 17, 2015

MAYER WISOTSKY

Seeing Me

People think of me, once in a while,
People think of me,
And sometimes smile.
I like to imagine what they see,
But I don't think it looks like me.
The Real me…the private me,
(That me that feels
The barbs of hateful criticism).
That me that wants to love humanity,
But hates the way they all behave.
How can I let you know I love you,
When your actions speak of bitterness and fear?
And do you care?
Should I care?
Do I dare to break the mold of civilization?
To tread on tradition and rearrange the social norms?
To show you that I care?

Come sit beside me,
Close your eyes and look at me
…and see me as I really am.

November 28, 2016

Compared to What?

How good can things be
If you have never been sad?
If things have never been bad?
If you have never cried
When you lost a friend,
How full could your life have been?
If you never lost a race,
Or been challenged by a hopeless task?
The greater the ecstasy
The deeper the sadness at its loss.
Life is always,
"Compared to What?"

March 17, 2019

MAYER WISOTSKY

DIFFERENCE

The last time I saw God
Was yesterday.
When I looked into the mirror.
He was right behind me.
She was all around the room.
They were in the air around me.
I was not alone,
I was connected, I was engaged,
I was part of…I was all of…
I was just my silly old self.
One stroke of a very thin pen,
One speck of a very bright color,
Just a piece of the wonderful beauty,
Of being alive.
I make a difference for what's to come.

June 17, 2019

JUST ME

I look to find,
But nothing changes.
I am too lazy in my looking.
Things are never like they're supposed to be.
Or is it just me?
Maybe I am looking in the wrong places?
Or am I too content to see?
I want to be happy, but I don't know how.
The world is not what I want it to be.
Or is it just me?
Who can help a fellow stranger,
When the stranger doesn't want to know.
Whose happiness is more important anyway?
Or is it just me?

June 18, 2019

MAYER WISOTSKY

Morning Meditations

Living, loving, and laughing
At a cruel world that gives me no clue
As to where my fortunes lie.
What am I supposed to do?
A world that slaps me up side my head,
And praises me for how well I stand the pain.
So I live and love and laugh.
What else is there to do?
The enemy is within me
And I cannot get it out.
How can I change thousands of years,
Of stupidity that comes with being born?
Who asked me to be born anyway?
There is something going on that I don't understand,
Moving me from bad to worse
Yet I cannot give up the life I live.
Who keeps giving me all these problems?
Forget it. I give up.
I will go back to
Living, and loving, and laughing
In the only world I know.

November 25, 2019

THE LEGEND OF THE TWILIGHT OWLS

I Am Not a Symbol

We live in a world of words,
Symbols of the reality we feel.
Symbols turn us on--they turn us off,
They control our understanding.
Yet we love symbols because
They are ours--no one else's.
Symbols and symbols of symbols,
That's what I have become.
I cannot find the real Me
Anymore,
The Me behind the symbols.
The Me I wish to love.

December 10, 2019

MAYER WISOTSKY

Once in a Lifetime

The world, my world, is wet.
It has rained the whole night long.
It cleaned the air of dust and debris,
But it didn't clean me.
It didn't take my worries away,
Or reverse my bad luck.
It did not take my pain away,
The pain of not knowing
What the daylight would bring.
Am I ready for whatever is sent my way?
Am I prepared for a life of chaos?
Why can't I enjoy the surprise of a new adventure?
Am I old and the years have taken their toll?
All this questioning from a little bit of water,
But the moment I have just lived,
Is gone and I didn't make it mine.
I must feel each moment
Make it mine.
For each moment comes,
But once in a lifetime
And I cannot let it slip me by.

December 11, 2019

Being Me

Life is burning in my breast.
When shall I rest? When shall I nest?
So much to do--so much to know.
So little time to make dreams come true.
How did I get here? Did I follow a plan?
I am the product--the end result,
But how did I get here? What path did I choose?
Or did someone else choose for me,
Telling me where to go.
I think I know (or almost know)!
No one taught me how to say No!
I thought you needed permission,
To oppose the social flow.
Life is burning in my chest,
I want to live my passions every day,
Letting my actions reflect my dreams.
I cannot see if the end is near,
I cannot say there is nothing to fear.
I must just keep being me,
Doing it big, letting the whole world see.

January 10, 2020

MAYER WISOTSKY

One Life

I am sad when people die,
Especially those who had never really lived,
Not because they died,
But because they hadn't really lived.
Being alive is a challenge,
And an obligation.
It takes guts and a lot of commitment
To fully live your life.
It takes rational thinking
And deep emotional feelings
To give your life its everlasting value.
It takes courage to be
Who you want to be,
To be the leader of your many selves,
Your many desires…your many obligations.
Living is a fine Art.
You have but one life to live,
Live it with style…a style all your own.

March 28, 2020

Ain't Life Grand?

I live in a world of Maybes
I dream of a world of Shouldbes
While I build a world of Willbes
Which was picked from a group of Couldbes
Oh my! Choices galore!
Ain't life grand!

April 8, 2020

MAYER WISOTSKY

Hello Happiness

There is power, there is strength
In every move we make,
There is beauty, there is grace
In how we face the questions
That we face.
We try to see the world
As a place both good and wise,
Where decisions are made for us to follow
Even when their meanings go unsaid.
We read our desire into every experience,
We see ourselves as the goal
Of all that is happening,
In the entire World…
And sometimes in the entire Universe.
But Reality is not here for us alone,
It encompasses all of us.
So let us use our power and strength
To link our worlds in every way.
Joyfulness can only be
If You are alive and connected
Making sure the world is coming too.

April 13, 2020

Independently Connected

Life seems fragile when you're old and grey.
Every moment is seen with fear:
Be careful, go slowly, there is no rush
To be alive.
Life can be felt in every moment,
If you stop to wonder why--
Why the sun keeps on shining,
Even though it's older than I can conceive.
Being alive is being full of vitality,
Eagerness to live another day,
Ready to pay the price for it.
Grab your partner, grab a friend,
Or just another person on the street.
Give them a hug, share the vitality of being alive.
You are connected
To everything that lives!
Life is still good, enjoy it with pleasure.
Whatever your age.

May 11, 2020

MAYER WISOTSKY

My Life

I tried to be my mother's boy,
My father's son, my sister's brother,
But who I really was…
I did not know.
I looked for me in other's eyes,
But all I saw was their need for me.
So I grew as a tree, without purpose,
Roots everywhere, branches wildly waving,
Following the sun and seeking water.
It was then I saw my mirror of hope.
I saw myself as another person
With all the options
I thought only other people had
And suddenly I realized
I could be whatever I wanted to be!
And so began the regrowing
Of My Life.

August 3, 2020

Two Sons

I have two sons
Who don't talk to me,
Because their pain is
Deeper than their understanding.
They were pawns in
A marital chess game,
Sacrificed to protect a Queen,
Or the King.
Now they wander in a world
Of misunderstanding,
Unable to heal the sorrow,
Unable to enjoy the belonging,
That they long for,
Unable to know their place,
As adults in an adult world.
How can I help them?
How can I try?
In their eyes I am the reason
For their discontent.
I have two sons,
But they don't have me.

August 25, 2020

MAYER WISOTSKY

Human Kind

I am what I am and more.
I am what I can be and have been,
Part of everything I see,
Everything I encounter,
Leaving my imprint on all I touch.
Becoming part of everything I've done,
Part of everyone's life I've met.
A bridge for those who need one,
A shoulder to cry on,
For those in pain.
Humanity is my middle name,
I am here for those who need me.
Humankind is my family.

August 25, 2020

THE LEGEND OF THE TWILIGHT OWLS

I Was There

Each morning when I wake,
I question who I am.
Inventory my existence…of what I have become.
I try to see the value of everything I have done.

What a waste of energy.

It is not what I have done,
Or will do,
But what I am doing.
This precious life,
Like a sliver of light,
Tearing through the black
Of a moonless sky,
Bringing understanding to my world.

Each morning I make a commitment:
I shall live each moment,
I will be there,
I will remember this day,
Because I was there…
I made it so.

September 27, 2020

MAYER WISOTSKY

Dumb Things

If you do dumb things,
You get stupid results.
Stupid results give you
False facts of reality.
Which leads to doing more…
Dumb Things.
An endless cycle of false facts
And dire circumstances…
Usually Death.
Think before doing,
Analyze what was done.
Learn from mistakes
And your problems will make you free.
Free to choose the life you want.

October 3, 2020

My Little Voice

I don't know what I don't know,
But my body does…
And is always telling me so.
My genes know what to say and do.
But do I listen to them?
I ask myself…Do I care?
The world is like a candy store
Temptation greater than I can bear.
But I must listen to that little voice
Crying in the middle of the night,
Begging for understanding
From anyone who will care,
For the little voice of me.
That makes my life worthwhile,
Makes me want to try.
Where are the mentors that were promised me?
Where is the reality I was meant to see?
All you get are guys
Who are trying to sell you crap that you don't need.
Get off of your knees little voice of mine,
And find the future of who you would be.

October 15, 2020

MAYER WISOTSKY

Pride

I was created by my mother's love,
And my father's lust.
A seed among the many,
Looking to be born.
(Connected to) An egg of plenty,
Waiting to be fertilized.
The combination became my journey.
Nothing special, no questions asked,
No tests of viability--no surety of success.
Life without a goal…Except survival.
I was born helpless,
Crying for my mother's breast.
And all I am is my mother's loving care,
And my father's strength.
Only now as I look back,
Through my many years,
I understand what they gave me.
I will make them proud of what I am.

October 23, 2020

The Cure

Why put a barrier in the road to understanding?
Because if you know…you must act,
Or your credibility is gone.
You cannot stand by and let someone die
Without knowing the reason.
So stop giving reasons for why you can't act,
Can't find a reason? Or don't know the facts?
If you can't begin acting
Get out of the way.
For those of us who care,
Are making our voices heard.
Incompetence in leaders is curable:
Get new leaders.

October 27, 2020

MAYER WISOTSKY

Falling Alone

I was born with the fear of falling
And the fear of being alone.
Even though I had no idea
Who "I" was.
The world presented itself to me,
In the form of food,
Soft shoulders and strong arms.
Calming my fears with sweet sounds,
And little kisses upon my head.
I was born naked in every sense,
And someone, called my parents,
Covered my body with warmth
And tenderness.
I didn't have to do a thing
But enjoy and complain.
I clothed myself as time went by,
With stories of monsters,
And dreams of how everything works.
I grew up trying to understand,
What the world was really like.
But to this day I am still trying
Not to fall or be alone.

November 27, 2020

Begin Again

In the Winter when it is cold,
I contemplate my past.
I think about growing old.
In the Summer when the sun shines,
I play in the Present with delight,
With little regard for my life passing by,
But in the Springtime
I am full of life,
Running in every direction,
Full of ideas and plans for the Future.
And then the Autumn
(the dreaded time of year),
Comes upon the scene.
I feel the pain of being born,
The commitment to stay alive,
When everything around me is dying,
Exploring my courage to see another Springtime.
A new life.
Arising from the litter of the dead.
This lesson learned or lessons spurned,
Your life goes on
And you start all over again.

November 28, 2020

MAYER WISOTSKY

My Mess

Little strips of paper
Strewn Upon My Desk,
Lines of poetry scribbled
On their faces.
Ideas crumpled on the backs of envelopes
(used of course)…
"What a mess" you say,
But like the mighty oak
From an acorn grows,
My poetry emerges.
My life of discovery,
My works of understanding,
Gave birth to
The Philosophy
of my Seeking soul.
And all around me
A "mess" is created,
By the unfolding of my life.

November 30, 2020

Mishpucha (Family)

In the Family of my friends,
I find contentment,
With people who have chosen to love me.
We have exchanged pieces of our being.
With each other.
We like the nearness of our bodies.
We like the feeling of our concerns.
The nature of our pasts intrigues us.
Our different upbringings fascinate us,
Cementing our feelings of love and affection
For one another.
Blood relatives are mandatory relationships.
Friends are choices of the heart.

December 13, 2020

MAYER WISOTSKY

Lies

Like gravitons of happiness
We rush to find our place
In a fractured world of discontent.
"Where do I belong"
In the name of right?
Or the name of wrong?
Does what I do matter
To the ever-emerging future?
Is the past worth repeating,
If I don't know what I have learned?
Questions that need facts…
Facts that need truth…
Truth that is based on trust…
Trust that has been destroyed
By lies.
A past full of lies…
Is a future full of chaos.

January 13, 2021

Eternal Me

You did not design your body,
Didn't even know you had one,
Till you were old enough to think.
But here you are stuffed into this body,
Wondering how did I get this way?
What can I do to change?
Then you realize…
I am more than my body:
There is a me beyond me,
A spirit…an essence…A bundle of reality…
Vibrating in the Real World.
This I can design, this I can mold and create,
If I have the desire…
The fortitude, the tenacity,
And the willingness.
I can be more than I am,
The eternal me.

March 7, 2021

MAYER WISOTSKY

Stolen Soul

You are not alone
In a crowded world.
Take that as a given.
So you must believe everything
You see and do
Is going to make somebody mad,
Or somebody sad,
It may even make somebody glad.
So what am I to do?
To get along…be part of the throng,
Right or wrong…
Who must I please?
I am turning into an automaton…
A silly drone…A bashful bot
Who hasn't got a lot to say.
I must get along, that's true.
And it's better than dying for an unjust cause.
Where is my mortality?
Did someone steal my soul?

March 19, 2021

THE LEGEND OF THE TWILIGHT OWLS

What's the Price?

Life is dynamic…moving…changing…
Never standing still.
Never saying you made it…
You've arrived…you've found perfection.
Perfection is always two steps ahead.
You are dynamic…moving…changing…
Never standing still.
Which one is changing which?
Can I stay--can I go?
Which feeling must I obey?
If I am wrong
What price will I pay?
Be brave…Jump into Life's
Whirling pace.
Enjoy the ride,
The price is just the same,
Whither it's pleasure or it's pain.

April 15, 2021

MAYER WISOTSKY

Your Life

Oh! For a life where all your dreams come true,
Where everything you do,
Makes you happy…brings joy.
A child's world of make-believe,
Where everything is alive,
Telling you of its plight
Or its happiness or its sorrow.
The real world is made with a fork in every road,
Always a choice…
Decisions to be made…
Consequences to be faced.
More decisions to be made…
"Down with decisions!"
Up with…
"I don't care anymore!"
Being an adult is a hard way to go,
If you want a life with meaning.
**YOUR LIFE IS A STATEMENT
OF HOW THE WORLD SHOULD BE!**

April 24, 2021

THE LEGEND OF THE TWILIGHT OWLS

Born Ignorant

What do I know?
I am just a human being,
Born in a world already begun.
Millions of years of evolution have passed
And along comes me.
What do I know?
I was born ignorant…
No understanding of how things work,
Of how I understand
Who I am.
My systems must be tested,
My curiosity must be fed.
My understanding must fit someone else's
Way of being.
I must go through many changes
Just to know how to search…
How to use someone else's searching…
How to know what to keep…what to cast aside,
Just to get through my teens.
What do I know? I don't know,
But I am going to find out now!

April 24, 2021

WHO ARE THEY?

Poems about who and what
Touches your soul
And judges your morality

MAYER WISOTSKY

A Parent

Sometimes I am all things to my child;
Sometimes I am nothing.
It is difficult to know when what I do,
Is what I should.
If against my breast, my child can beat out his anger
And then lay his head down upon me for love and warmth.
My child can become…
To flourish as his own being.
I must be his limits and his distant horizon.
I must be his future and his past.
I must be the paradox of life
And the absoluteness of death.
And if I am myself to him,
He will find himself in me.
Though I will forever be his parent,
He will go on to maturity.

1976

The Grasshopper

His skin is his exoskeleton,
His wall against the cruel, cold,
And dangerous world…
But it also keeps him from growing.
So when growth is necessary,
He must molt--shed his skin--
Destroy his wall, his past, and his security.
Then he is vulnerable to nature's whims.
But his fear is worth the trade…
Now, he can grow,
Expand and become greater in every way.

Be like the Grasshopper as you grow
And dare to tear down your walls of security.

1977

MAYER WISOTSKY

The Will

I seek the will to live.

That makes my seeking count,

The impetus that makes me want to try

When hopelessness abounds…

I need to have the energy,

To make it so,

When discontent won't let me go.

I crave the strength that makes me move,

When I am told to search for answers

To the questions I impose,

To questions yet unsaid.

To wishes that will yet unfold.

May 17, 2008

I Can't Let Life Pass Me By.

Is there beauty if no one experiences it?
Can there be love if no one receives it?
Is there reality without illusions?
Can there be purpose without destiny?
Is there a me without an us?
Can I be alone in a world full of people?
Can I be connected in a world full of loneliness?
Can any of these questions help me find a path to happiness?
I am in a quandary.
And I don't know why.
What I do know is:
I cannot let life pass me by.

May 7, 2012

MAYER WISOTSKY

A Song for the Faint of Heart

I am at the center of the essence of nothingness,
Empty and void in a meaningless life.
Where is reality when you need it?
There is no reality in my center,
Just an illusion of the "wannabes" of my past.
My parents' past…
My culture's past,
My, My, all is My…
But I have no My--just theirs--Others,
Both living and dead…
They are me, or I am them…
Where! Oh, where! Oh, where will it end!
Where am I now?
>Come play with me. You are my reality.
>My cocoon is waiting-- come in and lie with me,
>Pretend you really care.

April 8, 2014

Reflection Is My Path

Why would I share with a stranger
I'd never seen before?
Why would I help the traveler
Who comes knocking at my door?
What would make me reach out
To the poor and starving souls?
If I didn't see my reflection,
In the sorrow of their woes?
I am them and they are me,
We are all part of Humanity's mixture.
Rationality is no guide;
Practical reasons make no sense.
Reflection is my only path when the time for action comes.
I am you--we are one.
If Life is worth living for me,
It is worth it for everyone.

April 25, 2014

MAYER WISOTSKY

Creators

And there it was,
Me (the woodcarver), God and a piece of wood.
"**Nice piece of wood**," God said, "**I made it.**"
What do you mean you made it, I said.
You just started the process--
Everything else was automatic-- left to chance.
"**Don't forget--I Am chance**" God said.
Maybe so, but that's not creating with intention or purpose.
"**Are you creating with purpose**?" God asked.
Sometimes, I said, and sometimes I just let the wood guide me,
Just enjoying the way I feel cutting into the wood,
Or how the wood looks as I cut out a chip.
"**Sounds to me like there is more than just a purpose involved**," God noted. "**That sounds a lot like what I do.**"
Technically, I don't think you need a purpose
to create beauty.
"**Who judges anyway?**" God asked.
Good question, I responded, maybe just me.
"**I feel the same way**," God said.
The wood said nothing.

September 23, 2015

A Parent's Duty

"Tell me what is right and what is wrong,
Ask me to be kind--ask me to be strong,
Give me all the tools you think,
Will make me a real man.
Then send me out into the world,
To make it better if I can."
This is what parents do to satisfy their guilt,
For not making the world
What they thought it should have been.
Don't leave it to your children
To do what should be done.
Do it yourself and do it now,
A lesson to your children in understanding how.
Live life the way you want it to be--not the way it appears.
And your children will have a better world,
No matter what their fears.
Be a better person than you think
You already are,
And the world will applaud what you do
And your children will love you,
For who you are.
They will follow your example
Even if they never thank you.

January 4, 2020

MAYER WISOTSKY

Maturity

Who are all these voices
Claiming to own my soul?
Where did they come from?
There is one who sounds like my father
Another my mother…my aunt, my teacher…
All crowded in my head,
Telling me what to do, where to go,
How to act,
What to know.
Who pays for all these decisions?
Who pays the toll?
'Tis I, gentle people--it is me.
I am responsible for all the choices.
I am the one who pays.
Get out of my head, you voices of doom.
If I am to pay, the choice is mine!
I will decide what is right or is wrong.
Good-bye voices of the past?
You are only memories!
I am now in charge of Me.

January 21, 2020

Contagious

Did you laugh today?
Well you should have.
Did you love today?
Well you could have.
Did you treat the day with
Determination?
Making it a good day to be alive?
No one is keeping track of you,
Nobody is writing a book about you,
But they could have…
They should have!
Because when your life is great,
And you feel wonderful to be alive,
You are contagious!
And a lesson for us all.

March 28, 2020

MAYER WISOTSKY

Fear

Fear is never far away
In the natural world, they say.
Life comes and goes on its merry little way:
Things get eaten…things get born.
Things will change,
Pleasure will turn to pain,
Happiness to despair.
We are human when
We show we care.
Smile upon your fellow beings,
Help them salve their fears.
All this will last just a little while.
A new normal will arise,
And everyone will praise its value,
And lose their fears with yesterday,
Then bask in the new day's sun.
Reality is where you are my friend
Not where you are from.

April 28, 2020

THE LEGEND OF THE TWILIGHT OWLS

Go with the Moment

There is no promise you can make
That will guarantee the future.
So why should I listen to what you say?
Or follow your directions?
Everything is a guess.
What do you know about guessing?
I go by what I feel…
By what stirs my heart…
What satisfies that ache in my guts.
Can I look at you and know
The truth in what you say?
Or must I worry you don't know?
It is what it is.
I go with the moment.
I live it--it is all I have.

May 18, 2020

MAYER WISOTSKY

Eternity Without Time

The world knows no sadness
Only various degrees of joy,
But human beings can change even the best of things,
They can make even the smallest joys into tragedies,
The cycles of Life and Death must become
The destruction of goodness,
And the tearing away of enjoyment.
All Life must have destiny
Living can't be just living,
Purpose, accomplishment, reaching goals,
Leaving something behind after you have gone,
Why can't rewards be the process?
Existence only in the moment,
Eternity without time,
Reality without substance,
Feeling without judgment.

September 2010

THE LEGEND OF THE TWILIGHT OWLS

Group of One

If you are what you want to be
You have crossed the Great Divide:
That line between living
And watching other people live.
When you are young,
The secret of existence is your quest.
In Mid-Life,
The living of that secret is your challenge.
But in Old Age,
The helping of others to find their secrets
Is your duty and contribution.
You are only limited by the fantasies
Of your culture,
The truths held dearly by those
Who have come before you.
Is Good behavior doing
What you have been told to do?
Is Bad behavior breaking away,
Finding your own truth,
Deciding on your own direction,
Taking Responsibility for your life?
With no regrets?
You may only be a group of one
But that one will be the one you picked.

October 14, 2020

MAYER WISOTSKY

All I Am

If all I am is the color of my skin,
You have not gone deep enough.
If all I am is a myth of the God I choose,
You have not looked wide enough.
If all I am is the gender you perceive
You do not understand enough.
We are complex organisms,

(We Humans, not easily understood,
Lie to ourselves most of the time,
About who we are and why we do what we do.)

Reality is a partial truth,
Of who I am, of who you are.
How do I know what I know?
You are always more than
You think you are.
Forget my skin,
My myths,
My gender.
Know me for how I make you feel.
Know me by my essence.

November 4, 2020

A Part of You

You are but one among many,
But you're the only one who counts.
No one else cares about you 24 hours a day,
Thinks about you All the time.
So you must make the choice
Of how to live your life:
Making yourself happy…
Making yourself sad.
Sounds easy when you start out,
It's harder along the way.
Can't help others
Till you help yourself.
You must be a whole person
Before you can give part away.

November 23, 2020

MAYER WISOTSKY

Your Real Name

No one understands me,
No one cares about my feelings.
They tell me my feelings are wrong…
Invented, wishful thinking.
Should I listen to them?
They are judging me
Without my permission!
Can they do that?
Only if I let them:
"If you let other people define your reality you have none."
You must go into the world
And find your Real Name,
The person you were meant to be:
The only one who can truly judge
Your existence.

December 23, 2020

Every Morning

You must be yourself every day;
Do you know who you are?
What you have been?
Your effect on others?
You are a power house!
Poised to do something great!
Can you feel that?
Every morning you must say,
"Today I make a difference"
"Today my life has meaning"
"Somebody smiled and felt better
Because of me."
(And I felt better because they felt better)
And life goes on…
You make a difference.
Keep it up:
The world needs you…
I need you…
You need you!

January 30, 2021

LOVE

Poems that challenge your ability
To share your soul
Without losing your reality

MAYER WISOTSKY

IGNITE MY SOUL

As a summer's dawn brightens soft and warm,
As a cool sea breeze blows steady and calm,
As a lazy hawk glides easily in the skies,
I gaze upon you with love in my eyes.
I touch your being with my
outstretched soul.
I grope in your loneliness
for a spark of love.
And your glowing embers warm
And kindle my essence,
Igniting my soul.
I blaze with passion
In the calm serenity of your arms.
My body aches with desire
And my mind sails on the wings of fantasy.
I devour your image and taste the ecstasy,
Of all your charms.

1979

THE LEGEND OF THE TWILIGHT OWLS

For Me It Is You

For one person, love is sweet,
For another, it is sorrow.
For the moon, it is a lament.
For the sun, it is tomorrow.
For me it is you.

You have touched my soul,
My essence,
My being

September 9, 1979

MAYER WISOTSKY

Many is the Mile

Ten, twenty, many is the mile
I travel from you,
But Love is flying
Filling the space,
So that being apart
Is never more than
The thought of your smile,
And the warm memories,
Of your embrace.

June 9, 1984

The MOON

The Moon is neither green nor blue,
The Moon is the color of your hair,
For it shines about your face each day,
And brightens the world I share.
           You are soft and gentle as a Moon should be,
           Brightening all of the world you see,
           And when you look at me--I brighten too,
           Your presences enthralls me,
Touches me in a way that lasts beyond my control,

I shall love you always, for I have no choice,
You are the Moon of my darkest night--
The possesor of my
Soul.

June 1993

MAYER WISOTSKY

Friendship

Bit by bit, the story builds,
Piece by piece the truth appears,
Slowly, I become who I am,
Who I was--who I want to be.
I grow as a person, bit by bit.
Am I the person you want me to Be?
So who am I to you?
Am I but one cog in the machine of your mind?
I offer a choice--an idea--an example--or a direction.
I must be weighed, compared, analyzed, and tried.
 Then I must be incorporated or discarded;
 Once incorporated I must be used.
Only then will wisdom begin,
When we intertwine and feed each other,
Acting as parents, one to another.
 Thus, life has meaning,
Existence a goal.
Being becomes truly Being
In the shaping of our Souls.

August 12, 2013

The Smiling Faces

There are times when the moon shines brightly,
And my dark, lonely nights look happy.
There are times, in a cloud-filled sky,
When the sun peeks through and brightens my world.
There are people whose gloomy sadness,
Is changed by a joyful smile,
A moment transformed by joy,
That makes the monotonous day worthwhile.
I love those people with the smiling faces.
I envy their cheerful abandoning of life's inevitable chores.
I wonder if I can smile my chores away,
And be irresponsibly happy the rest of my days.

February 19, 2014

MAYER WISOTSKY

Mourning Dove

In the morning as I sipped my tea,
I heard a dove cooing quietly outside my window,
Or so it seemed,
His little cries of simple pleasure to be alive,
Enjoying his being.
That's what he seemed to say to me,
And I was glad I was alive,
I was happy I was here,
Enjoying the world I did not know,
Learning from a bird what gives me pleasure.
In the morning, my tea tastes good,
The day will be wonderful,
As it should.

May 3, 2014

Octogenarians

Is there something in the years that mitigates your fears?
Let you know you've been where fools have tread,
And yet you realize you've made some reasonable moves,
Because you're still alive--not dead?
Experiences have a way of adding up,
As long as you're not giving up,
To let you know that life is full of hope,
And every minute had its chance to be a moment of joy,
To prove your existence is definitely worthwhile.

February 15, 2015

MAYER WISOTSKY

Legacy

The wind shifted, a cloud lifted, I can see the sun again.
The world is bright, my goal in sight, everything looks just great.
Why then must I continue in this silly helpless plight?
Inside my body ticks a little clock, ticking away the minutes of my days,
Telling me time is here forever, but I could never be.
So I must do what must be done today, before it is too late--
Before my body will return, to the place from whence it came.
The game of life is not a game; the stakes are way too high--
A misstepped step or a silly left could end my mortal being.
Yet I must take the giant leap and throw myself to the wolves,
Hoping that their stomachs are full from eating other fools.
The world will persist with or without me, this I know for sure,
But I can leave some memories in the minds of many,
That makes their lives more livable
When thinking on where I've been.
So jump I must and jump I will--into the fire of life's demands,
and I shall burn with such a flame
And my existence will have such a glow
That all the tomorrows that will follow me,
Will have nowhere to go.

September 24, 2015

We Are

We are,
But what we are
As we are becoming,
What we shall be,
We will see what we will be,
When we really want to see it,
And
We will feel what can be felt
When we have felt that
Which rises from our souls.

Together we go beyond
Together we shall know no bounds
We shall be what we shall be
With our love of what we are.

May 15, 2017

MAYER WISOTSKY

Life Is for the Living

Don't take Life for granted,
Just because you're living it.
It could be gone at any time,
By a wrong turn or faulty wire,
A cigarette butt on a windy day.
Every second is precious--sacred--
And profound.
Yet how do we face it?
With joy or trepidation?
Eagerness or resentment?
Depression or excitement?
Your attitude matters.
Your understanding is your road map.
Don't take Life for granted.
It is the only thing you have in common,
With all other living things.
Love it--cherish it.
Treat it with care
Live it as Royalty.
Not in despair.

November 12, 2018

THE LEGEND OF THE TWILIGHT OWLS

To Love! To Love!

We pledge our yearning souls
To live and love and make our futures
Joyous.
But a single bird cannot create alone,
So being one can never satisfy,
And being together means giving your heart,
Then soothing the hurt the giving has done.
Are we separate when we feel we are one?
Or are we just two people thinking we are one?
Oh! To love with all that it means!
To reap all the heartaches,
And still feel that love.
Being happier than a human can be--
This is where I belong.

2019

MAYER WISOTSKY

Unique You

For every tomorrow there is a yesterday,
That keeps us from enjoying today.
You are a three-dimensional person,
Casting two-dimensional shadows,
Wherever you may go.
But time flows in only one direction,
Every minute of the day.
So, you must grab each second of life,
Forgetting that time exists.
You must be in eternity's space,
Living life with a sense of Awe.
Feeling the world in the depths of your soul,
Sharing with your fellow human beings,
The joy of being alive.
For you are unique,
A once-in-a-lifetime phenomenon.
You shall never be again.
Love yourself for your uniqueness,
And others for their recognition of it.
Never stop learning who you are becoming.

September 10, 2019

THE LEGEND OF THE TWILIGHT OWLS

For Opal Irene Wisotsky
(born March 11, 2020)

The sweetness of tomorrow,
Shining in this little face,
Showing all the world
A new beginning has begun.
Let no one doubt this little heart,
Will beat with fervor and resolve,
And change the lives of many,
With the beauty she will bring.
Many will be touched,
By the brilliance of her understanding.
Her love will be in everyone's heart,
As she helps humanity grow.
She is a sign of a better world
A better place to be.
The changing color of an Opal's being
Will be the brilliance of her world.

Great-grandpa
March 11, 2020

MAYER WISOTSKY

Being You

You are who you are
Because you think you are.
Your brain is telling you so.
Your body will obey,
If it thinks you are serious,
If you are willing to be consistent
In your desire to reach your goals.
It takes discipline; It takes resolve.
Most of all it takes truth,
Honesty with self,
No lies for any reason.
You are who you want to be
When you are the leader of your life,
When you are in charge,
When you are responsible.
No scapegoating with phony explanations,
You are you because you decided to be you.
And You are Wonderful!

April 6, 2020

Loving is Living

Loving is living
And living is real.
It's what caused babies to coo
And children to laugh.
It is the connections to others
Whether you know them or not.
It brings great satisfaction
When the loving is returned.
So, look to your neighbors,
And family and kin,
With a sense of belonging
An emotion within.
If you are living you are loving,
And it feels oh so good!

February 21, 2021

LONELINESS

Poems about the implosion of your world
That separates you from humanity
While craving their connections

MAYER WISOTSKY

Life Is Not a Lonely Happiness

Throughout life you are concerned,
With only one person all of the time.
You feel all things singularly,
(even collective behavior)
You reach out occasionally
And touch another person,
Share another's soul.
But only for a moment.
Then you take that moment of bliss,
Rush it back to your solitude
And savor its minutest details,
Feeling and re-feeling that touch of ecstasy.
So,
When you reach out
   And see yourself in someone else's eyes,
When you cry
   And someone else's tears begin to fall,
When you tremble with enjoyment
   And someone else begins to laugh,
You will know your moment has come
And you will never be lonely again.

1977

THE LEGEND OF THE TWILIGHT OWLS

A Part of Someone Else's Life

I am alone in a world full of people,
And I try, with all my might,
To be a part of some one else's life,
But I cannot.
I think and I think, but I cannot feel,
And in my dreams, both day and night,
Everyone becomes a part of my life,
My needs--my wants--my wishes,
And as my dreams fade,
Reality defines my pain,
The longing for my mother's warmth,
For the nourishment of my soul.

June 22, 2007

MAYER WISOTSKY

The Dilemma

I was born in a particular time.
I did not pick my birth, nor create my life,
But I am responsible just the same.
Like it or not.
All the world spread out before me.
And I must make the choice.
All I know is what I've been told,
Yet I must make the choice
I did not ask to be here.
I do not have a goal.
But I must make the choice,
Of how to guide my soul.

February 21, 2014

THE LEGEND OF THE TWILIGHT OWLS

The Poet's Inspiration

I cannot seek what does not call,
I cannot speak of conquering all,
I am but a small and insignificant man,
Adrift upon an unforgiving sea,
Hoping for the sun to shine, praying for the wind to cease,
Wishing for a place to stand,
Longing for a piece of land.
Where are the **Powers** that rule the universe?
Can they not see that my feet are worn?
Can they not hear my cries of fear?
Must I become a robot to be free?
Free of thinking, free of choice,
Free of all the things that make a human be?
Make me real.
**Oh Powers that be--
Call to Me**

April 22, 2014

MAYER WISOTSKY

My Favorite Lies

Of all the lies I've told you in my life,
The one I like the best is the one that says,
"Lies don't hurt anyone for very long."
I was wrong,
My lies were reflections of what I wanted to be,
A wall of illusions to make me feel good,
The end of quests when I went looking for myself,
A tangle of fairytales with no happy endings,
A parcel of costumes for wearing disguises,
Masks for keeping me totally alone,
Alone with secrets of the false exploits
I never really had.
I lied to myself and this I regret.
Now,
I cannot judge which lies
I have already met.

April 22, 2014

THE LEGEND OF THE TWILIGHT OWLS

Youth's Painful Truth

I read the words, but not their intent.
I see the symbols, but not their implications.
I hear the sounds, but not their manifestation.
I taste a world of promised pleasure,
With no understanding of how to make it so.
I'm immortal, in transition to a place I do not know.
I am incomplete in every way, yet I must begin.
Alone I must make the trip,
Alone I must choose the ideas I take with me.
I must own the life I live,
And it is just me who must live it.

August 8, 2014

MAYER WISOTSKY

The Beginning of Belief

What dangers lurk beyond my door?
I don't know, but there will be many, many more.
What pleasures beckon my restless soul?
I know not and I fear there will be none!
I am without choice--I am without voice,
I fear the loneliness I must endure.
My backbone bends and turns like a pretzel.
I am afraid.
I am alone.
I must create illusions to help me through the day,
Illusions to keep me happy so that I may go on,
My dreams will get me through the night.
And I think I will awake if they are wrong,
I must create illusions that make me safe,
For I know my realities cannot
Rectify my mistake after mistake,
After mistake I'll make.

January 2015

THE LEGEND OF THE TWILIGHT OWLS

The Moral Compass

I walked through life with a little kind of swagger.
Tried to be a big man when I was younger.
People would say to me, "take your time, take it easy,"
But I was in a hurry to get what I thought was mine.
I took every shortcut I could see;
Ended up missing the learning that needed to be.
Life grew complex and all my lies became real.
I began to believe I was my illusions;
Deception was the middle name of my success.
Things didn't go well and I didn't improve…
It was then I realized my life was a disaster.
Who was to blame for this mountain of mistakes?
Who led me astray when I asked what it costs?
Who taught me to see the world in this stupid way?
I do not know. I cannot say. I walk the streets searching in vain,
Pondering
What made me so weak when I should have been strong?
A moral compass is that what you say?
Where do you buy one and what must I pay?

November 23, 2016

MAYER WISOTSKY

Good People

Some good people are born good people,
Some learn it through experience.
And then there are some,
Who seek a life of goodness,
Because they want to do
The right thing--
The thing that makes them
Truly human,
Caring about others
As they care about themselves.
Find a good person
And you will never be alone.
Find a good person
And your life will never be
Just your own.

Revised October 2, 2019

Wondering

I sit and wonder every day,
Just what makes me live my way.
Did I choose the path I tread:
Look for meaning?…Look for love?
Or was I told to be this way?
Or was it lies they told
(adults)
When I was young,
Believing everything they said?
How do I know that what I know is mine?
Or am I just a parrot,
Spitting out what I have heard,
Screaming out "I care,"
What they said?
I sit and wonder, mull it over,
Then I return to doing nothing.
For the rest of the day,
Feeling good about my wondering.

March 16, 2020

MAYER WISOTSKY

THE PLAGUE

And the days go by
And the moon still shines,
But I miss you, my friends,
My family…connections with my world.
The Plague has changed my life.
The brutal truth is much too harsh.
Why can't my lesson be gentler?
Death marches out each day,
To take its toll and shape my existence.
A virus smaller than I can see
Testing everyone's reason for being,
Teaching what can't be taught any other way.
How beautiful the world is when I awake.
How lonely without the people.
Shuttered away, I understand the beauty
I have no more.
Will I remember the lessons I learn?
If I still have a chance to learn them?

March 28, 2020

Feeling Alive

The days are growing longer.
There is music in the trees.
The birds are singing to one another.
Winter is sliding away.
Spring belongs to mothers
Everywhere feeding their young.
Flowers are reaching for sunshine
And bees are making honey.
How sweet it is.
And how sweet are you?
Can you embrace the morning full of love?
Can you feel the vibrancy of living
Flowing through your veins?
Are you up for feeling alive
In an exciting way?
Don't waste your life in hating,
Or bitterness;
It won't change anything.
Be always in the springtime of your life,
Blown away by the beauty
You are part of.

January 22, 2021

CHANGE

Poems that explore
The forces of time and growth
That change our lives

MAYER WISOTSKY

Change

Everything is Changing.
Growing up or growing old…
Everything is different, from second to second,
Hour to hour, year to year.
Change makes the world go 'round.
You can make Change your enemy…
Or your friend.
You can enjoy it or loath it,
But you cannot stop it.
It is what our understanding…Our existence…
And the life of our world…
Is all about.
To enjoy life, you must learn
How to change the changing world--
Giving new names to old ways,
Moving old furniture to new places,
Renaming old sites as new sights,
Now is always half way to somewhere
And the magic of growing up
Is called growing old.

December 20, 2020

THE LEGEND OF THE TWILIGHT OWLS

To Begin Again

Many years have passed and yet I grieve,
I grieve the passing of my youth.
Though I have no regrets,
I grieve the could-have-beens,
The might-have-dones,
What I almost became.
But what I learned…?
What I saw in the moments missed,
In the almost became,
In the nearly done,
That I cherish most of all.
So now I begin again.

April 21, 1979
revised July 31, 2020

MAYER WISOTSKY

The Last Poem In Oregon

This is the last poem I shall write in Oregon – as of Sunday
I will be a Californian once again.
What is it to separate? To break away and remove the force
that keeps you tied to a world of habit? Cut the bonds that
keep you bound
to one place--one time--one way of life.
What does it mean to leave?
But we are always leaving something:
Home in the morning…food on our plates…
Wakefulness at night … life before death.
You must always leave somewhere to get to someplace.
Leaving becomes the way to get somewhere.
The longest trip begins with leaving.
So it is with life:
(You must) leave childhood to become an adult--
(You must) leave your dependency to become free--
(You must) leave your ignorance to become wise--
(You must) leave your assumptions to find truth.
Let us celebrate our leaving,
Then our arriving can be filled with joy.

1990
Revised 2020

Time

Time, that miserable Bastard,
Creeping up
When life begins to look so
Beautiful
When the reasons for living
Become so clear.
Time, that robber of youth,
Cares not for your understanding
Your wisdom and appreciation
Of life.
It just keeps on going,
Rushing to Eternity
And leaving you behind.

March 17, 2003

MAYER WISOTSKY

Springtime
(Life is a joy for all who live it, a thrill for those who love it).

When bluebirds sing, Nature is everywhere,
When flowers bloom, Life is on the move.
Spring is the beginning of a journey.
I walk in search of realities, I seek,
I look for the proof of my existence.
I think I know who I am…I think…
I think I know where I'm going…
I thought I knew who I was…   where I had been…
but I didn't and I don't.
I walk as a blind man, tentatively,
Putting each foot carefully in front of the other,
Feeling for a solid path.
Though I do not know if that is the way…
The way I should go.
Second thoughts become third thoughts.
Then fourth thoughts…
Doubt clouds my eyes.
Trepidation swells in my chest;
It freezes me in my space.
I become immobile.
I wither as in Winter
I die.
But it is Spring!
I must be reborn!!!

January 3, 2013

Goodbye My Past

I am a definition of I know not what.
I think I have real meaning in someone else's reality,
Yet I have no "I" that I can see.... something that I can call
The real me?
Life is cruel in its unfolding, never letting me know its plan.
Disillusion upon dissolution is cast into my path,
And I spin like a drunken sailor to avoid the wrath.
I build an explanation for each crazy thing I do,
And my life becomes a model of a well directed plan,
An afterthought of wasted life--
Senseless life--full of regrets--full of lies--
Full of questions and unexplained "whys."
What must I do to find my being? To see--to feel--
My existence?
The question hangs like a Damocles sword,
Its answer cutting away my past
(From all the things I thought I loved so well,
From all the things that felt like living hell.)
"Goodbye my past." I must depart.
I must give up my lying heart--and start anew.
I must forge a life with no regrets, no illusions to sap
My strength,
A life of encounter--challenge and pursuit--
Being born every moment--being born without a past.

July 5, 2014

MAYER WISOTSKY

Life Times

What I see makes no sense to me,
For I am faced with life's great dilemma,
Life's ever nagging question:
What is it all about?
At the end of each and every day…
Does it matter what I do?
Does it really matter? And to whom?
Does it matter what I leave?
Does it matter what I conceive?
At the end of each and every hour…
Is there purpose in this real World?
Is there a destiny that will be revealed?
At the end of each and every minute…
This moment is my eternity.
It lives without my consent.
Yet I must live it, none the less,
For it will pass me by without delay,
As it breaks down everything into decay,
At the end of each and every second…
It needs no meaning to be born,
It needs no purpose to go on,

THE LEGEND OF THE TWILIGHT OWLS

We call it **Time** and think we understand,
As it marches triumphantly along.
But it is what makes up our lives,
At the end of each and every tick of Time…
Second after second, beckoning to us
To give it meaning, give it grace,
Make the memory worth a minute of reflection.
Making existence go beyond its space.
At the end of each and every tock of Time…
Your past will always follow you,
As you live each moment of your day,
So you must live it with the eagerness,
Of a newly hatched bird of prey,
Ready to spread your wings and fly,
Away to Eternity's endless point.
Where Time is but a passing thought,
In the accomplishments you will have brought,
At the end of your each and only life.

March 25, 2015

MAYER WISOTSKY

There Is No Forever Me

All my days are holy,
For I am on a holy quest,
To find the reason for my being.
I tried to find the Me
(the essence of my soul)
So I could build a life around it.
But as I aged, I realized I was not
A constant force--I was changing,
Every Day.
There is no Forever Me.
I must be born anew,
In the nowness of reality.

August 2, 2019

THE LEGEND OF THE TWILIGHT OWLS

Living Each Day

Watch the morning melt away.
Beg the afternoon to stay.
The day is slowly fading,
The evening about to begin,
And what have I done?
Nothing that amounts to anything,
You know.
But I was there when the blackness
Surrounded my soul.
When the night began to go.
I lived each moment of that whole day
Twenty-four hours of my life was done.
Now I am ready to enjoy
The morning melting into another day.

December 10, 2019

MAYER WISOTSKY

Face to Face

We live upon a world of unknowing
We wonder why we are so misunderstood,
We try to make sense of simple gestures
we think we know what makes it so.
But we forget just how we got there,
How we taught ourselves to think.
How we tested our crazy ideas of
What made the world round.
We bought the myths of others,
Then created some of our own:
Parking Spirits, Guardian Angels,
Santa Claus and Tooth Fairies.
We seem to think there is some reason,
Behind every move we make.
That there are no accidents in this complex world,
Just signs and messages of things to come,
But we cannot speak the language
The meaning is not clear
And the hearing aids of Religion
Only increase the volume not the clarity.

THE LEGEND OF THE TWILIGHT OWLS

We must find a linguist
Who is not a charlatan of the truth
or a soothsayer or a shaman
Or an intercessor to a God without reason,
Who can teach us the language
So we can see the truth
With our own eyes, hear it with our own ears,
Decide on it through our own understanding.
We must talk to God directly
Face to Face
Whatever Face he wears.

November 28, 2019

MAYER WISOTSKY

This Day

What day is this?
Or does it matter?
Every day is a day to live,
Not just to endure.
But to revel in the sacred feeling
Of being alive!
For if the day has just begun
You can be sure it will end,
And looking back
At how you spent the time,
Between beginning and the end.
The times you were unhappy,
The moments you were sad,
The stupid things you did, trying to be funny…
The silly things you did, trying not to be mad…
They all add up to the life you led.
Nothing can be changed. Nothing can be undone.
Let it go, "It is no more!"
Begin as the new day rises,
To make that day worth
The price you paid,
For the past you endured.

December 25, 2019

THE LEGEND OF THE TWILIGHT OWLS

Goals

There is no right or wrong without a goal,
A statement to measure against…
Compare to…
All life starts with a purpose.
Living life is a process,
Trying to reach that goal.
But every goal subordinates to a higher goal,
And the highest goal
(the one you got when you were born)
Is to Survive.
The living of life is the process.
This Is Where You Want To Be,
Where you want to live.
In this moment of time,
That second of regret,
That eternity of pleasure…
Good food, Good friends, Good loving,
Good searching for the Good life…
All good for nothing,
If you don't know who you are.
And why do you want to survive?
So what is your goal now?

August 22, 2020

MAYER WISOTSKY

Now and Never

Think you are wise?
Think you are clever?
Do you know the difference,
Between now and never?
Destiny waits for no one.
Don't put off your living,
For when things get better.
Live this moment (it may be your last).
If things in your life are wrong, change them.
If they can't be changed,
Begin again.
Be reborn, have a clean slate.
Now is the beginning of forever;
Never is nowhere to be found.

September 18, 2020

Become Again

I sit in the garden waiting
For the sun to shine its way to noon,
Watching the birds and squirrels
Eating breakfast on the run.
As I sip my tea, I think:
Life is so profound
And everything alive,
Moving…changing…becoming
Again and again.
And I must change with it, like the wind.
I must move on,
Change and become again,
No matter how old
I become.

October 12, 2020

MAYER WISOTSKY

Hair

The color of your hair changes,
As you grow older,
To remind you of your mortality.
It tells you that life
Constantly changes.
You must change too.
You must be challenged…
You must be thrilled…
A new you,
Relearning to laugh,
At the tough parts…
Cry at the sad parts…
No living in the past.
Let your hair remind you
Of where you are…
And where you ought to be.

February 2, 2021

THE LEGEND OF THE TWILIGHT OWLS

If

If you want to be loved,
Be loving.
If you want happiness,
Be laughing.
If you want remembrance,
Be giving.
If you want understanding,
Be patient.
If you want exploration,
Be risky.
If you want to enjoy life,
Be forgiving.
And if you don't want anything,
Just Be You.

March 11, 2021

DEATH

Poems about the value of Death
As a phenomenon of Life
And a factor for change

MAYER WISOTSKY

Memories Can Never Die

Life shines as a bright light
In the vast darkness called Death
Which is really just the Unknown.

Each life is like a beacon
Shrinking the darkness.
When the light of someone's life
Goes out,
We curse the darkness, the unknown--
Death.
We curse its inevitability,
For we know not what awaits us in the
Void.

Though life is but a measured time,
We live it as if it were forever--
So when the light of someone's life
Goes out,
And the darkness takes its place,
We are devastated.

Cry for what might have been,
Wail for the emptiness that is
Then remember all the beauty that was
And smile,

Memories can never die.

1987

A PIECE OF THE SOUL
(On the Death of My Aunt)

The world is a place to live and love,
To be related to things--to people,
To be part of a larger whole,
Connected with a living force,
But Death comes and separates
The darkness from the light.
To Death you must go alone,
All connections broken,
The end of the living force--
Togetherness gone,
Aloneness replacing love,
Emptiness in exchange for ebullient life,
Darkness for light,
Tomorrow for yesterday,
Death for life.
Yet I will not give up my yesterdays,
I will not forget my love-filled ways,
Death has the body,
But I have a piece of the soul.

1998

MAYER WISOTSKY

The Narrow View

When people die, you wonder why.
You feel some pain. You begin to cry.
You think you've lost a piece of your past,
Because things have changed in the world you cast.
Your status quo has gone berserk.
Your strategy for living will not work.
Your narrow view of life is shaken,
Because Death has proved it all mistaken.
Life is always just beginning,
Death is just around the bend,
You must follow life's path,
Living each moment to its end.

March 1, 2013

The End of It All

As the morning sun begins to rise,
And the lonely night has slipped away,
I dream the way the day will go,
But then again I do not know,
I do not know the depth of my sorrow,
I have lost so many loving souls.
People who helped define my life,
Lie beneath a marker stone,
So much of my happiness beneath the dirt,
So much of my life replaced by hurt.
I am the last of my little Clan,
No one to talk to about the past,
No one to question when you are the last…
"Do you remember that funny day?"
"What was his name, the guy down the block?"
"Did we have fun that day in the park?"
Memories I can no longer recall,
Because I am the last,
The end of it all.

July 17, 2013

MAYER WISOTSKY

About Death

One **good** thing about Death is that it gets rid of people you don't like.
One **bad** thing about Death is that it gets rid of the people you do like.
Another **good** thing about Death is that it reminds us that we are mortal,
When we experience somebody else's Death.
Another **bad** thing about Death is that it has to kill somebody,
In order to give that message.
Yet another **good** thing about death is that you can use it as a metaphor,
And get rid of parts of your past.
Yet another **bad** thing about death is that you have to start your life all over again.
Death is Sisyphus' **bad** rock that rolls back down the hill.
But it is your **good** rock that forces you—motivates you—
To push the rock up again,
That rock that is the living of your life.

August 23, 2014

Death Oh Death

Death shows no remorse. It has no regrets.
It does its job without a care,
Without caring
For the havoc it causes, for the guilt it instills,
And the sadness it creates in the living,
That it spares.

October 6, 2014

MAYER WISOTSKY

The Light of Living

In darkness we are born,
In darkness we will die,
But it is in the brilliant light of living,
We live our lives--we develop our ways,
And we think our thoughts.
Time to shine with the reflected light of all the energy around us,
Of all the people we encounter, all the love we lavish on one another.
Enjoy that force--that force of life--that desire to just be,
And then pass on all that enjoyment of living,
That joy of loving and being loved in return.
The darkness will always be there waiting--
No need to worry.
So let the light of living fill your days and nights,
and let the light of loving be your life's delights.

June 20, 2015

Alan's Father

Life is but a fleeting view,
of what the world could be,
and Death is but its misty door.
It opens to I-know-not-what,
but I know there must be more.
Your father came and spent his time,
then walked on through that door--
now his memories fill your life,
as your memory will ensure,
to share the feelings of his fleeting view,
of how your world could be,
by passing it on to all the world,
for everyone you see.

January 10, 2017

MAYER WISOTSKY

A World of Grey

A New Day has dawned upon the Earth,
And I am challenged to find its worth.
I sit and ponder what to do,
To find the greatness of this moment,
I have been given a formidable task,
To not waste a second of this precious life,
This sacred gift of being alive.
I watch those I love (or want to love)
Taken from my world.
The older I get the more people I see die.
I cry for their passing, still wondering why.
Is living life so hard that only through death,
We see its value?
Oh! What a price to pay!
I must work every day
Not to waste the gift of life:
Make life thrilling, not mundane.
I must be the symbol of joy,
In a world gone grey.

December 6, 2018

Survival

Survival is your first commitment.
Without it there is no Life,
Without Life there is no Hope,
Without Hope there is no Future,
Without the Future there can be no Present,
No present means no Past
Stay alive and all things are possible.
Courage is your steadying force,
Curiosity is your guide,
Memory is your classroom,
Where analysis teaches you Truth.
Your energy is a magnet,
For your desires,
Drawing things and people into your
Realm--your sphere of understanding.
Be respectful of the gift of Life,
Don't waste it on frivolous games,
For Death is always waiting,
For Survival to be misunderstood.

December 21, 2018

MAYER WISOTSKY

Alive in the Shadow of Death

Are we ever prepared to face the reality of Life?
In darkness we are born. In darkness we will die,

Or more specifically the reality of Death?

But it is in the brilliant light of Life
We live our lives—we forge our ways,
And we think our thoughts.

Death, that sobering experience of a final Action,
That irrevocable line of separation,
No more dreams of what's to come,
No more plans of what will be,
No more time to say or do
What should have been.

Time to shine with reflected light of all the energy,
Of all we encounter, of all the love we lavish on one another,

Reality is cruel--
It robs us of our illusions
It takes away our dreams
And does it in the form of
Death.

THE LEGEND OF THE TWILIGHT OWLS

Enjoy that force--that force of life--that desire to just be,
And then pass on all that joy of living,
That joy of loving and being loved in return.

But if Death is real so must Life be real
    And we must be in that reality:
        No Illusions--No Dreams
No Regrets--No Expectations. Death tells us to be real
    Death demonstrates our foolishness
        Death stops time, stops motion
        Death is the darkness of space.

The darkness will always be there, waiting--
No need to worry.
So, let the light of Life fill your days and nights,

To the dead Death has no meaning,
    To the living it is Profound,

And the light of loving will let you be
Alive in the Shadow of Death.

December 20, 2019

MAYER WISOTSKY

LAST TIMES

When I was young, trepidation had no meaning,
Caution had no value.
Profound changes of my life seemed a shallow reality.
I had to take charge of a world
I did not create,
Did not own and did not understand.
I had to become responsible for a life
I did not create,
In a world I hardly knew,
With rules I did not suspect,
Until I was punished for them.
(To this I must say "thank you" to the Gods of survival,
Who made me question the world)
And now, in my later years,
I must count, each time I encounter,
The Last Time I will do That,
Whatever That is,
The Last Time I do that.
"For I grow old, I grow old,
I shall wear the bottoms of my trousers rolled."
I'm Just beginning the many Last Times I must endure,
Still living the life I claim as mine.
Still loving the Joy,
Of being able to have one more last time.

May 10, 2019

THE LEGEND OF THE TWILIGHT OWLS

Every Day

We tarry as we Mingle
And marry Our Thoughts with Actions,
Carrying all our Baggage with Us
Into a Future where Truth is not our companion.
We look for Love, not from Above,
But from the ones who can least afford to give It.
We are Humans trying to be free,
Free of the fear that we someday will not be here.
Where will I be then?
Do not tarry--Life is short.
Live It with the Conviction
That there is a pattern
To be found.
And I am part of the Unity,
A stitch of Reality
In the fabric of The Void.
I hold It all together,
Keep It from unraveling.
Take Heart--you are needed
In your very special way.
Be who you are,
Every Day--Every Day--Every Day.

August 4, 2019

MAYER WISOTSKY

A LITTLE BIRD

Death has come and talked to me,
And told me to take care.
A little bird flew into my window,
And the sweet little brown bird
Fell upon the ground and died.
A broken neck or concussion of the brain,
I don't know which,
But in my hands, I watched him
Close his eyes,
And never a word was said.
I comforted him with gentle sounds,
And petted his sweet little head,
Hoping he would stay alive.
I must remember that seeing the truth,
Is not the same as living it.

October 7, 2019

Yahrzeit for Colleen

It's morning of the day,
One year ago, today.
There is mourning on this day,
One year has passed away.
Colleen Riggs is now a memory.
We sense her presence--we feel our pain.
We wish that we could talk to her again.
To tell her of the sorrow we have felt
Since she has gone away,
And let her know that her memory
Shall never fade away,
As long as we will live.
Rest in peace sweet Colleen,
You are immortal in our hearts.

November 8, 2019

MAYER WISOTSKY

DECIDEPHOBIA

In the morning glow of heavenly dew,
I saw the sun reflected.
I saw the colors from red to blue,
Bouncing in a drop of water.
I saw my life reflected in the myriad
Dewdrops on the grass,
All the possibilities
Spread out before me,
Begging me to choose.

All I could do was look,
And wonder at the future,
Not realizing I had a choice,
A decision to make it so.
But it's cold outside.
I think I will go
And make a cup of tea.

March 15, 2020

THE LEGEND OF THE TWILIGHT OWLS

PARADOX

Poems that create illusions
Of the unsolvable
Into solutions of the possible

MAYER WISOTSKY

Absolute Relativity

What makes the world go round,
Is the same thing that defines up from down,
The simple laws of reality,
That's what it is!
The same laws that define you and me.
A reality beyond our control,
But formed by our existence,
A paradox of truth,
A certainty of the moment--an ignorance of eternity,
A sense of being--an uncertainty of immortality.
Laws of level--Laws of position
Reality from a point of view,
Absolute Relativity.

1990

Price of Sanity

Puzzles of reality
Madness in the making,
Truths with shades of color
Shaking in their illusions.
Paradoxes of life,
Making us all crazy
Because we are all lazy.
Logic becomes the price
Of our sanity.
We use it to make our lives sane
Because we are lazy
And can't stand the pain.
Now our lives are wrapped up tight.
If it is not logical it's not right.
Oh! What a price we pay
To keep our illusions,
To keep the paradoxes away.
Sleep my children,
Death is a paradox
you won't understand
Until you are dead.

1999
Revised 2019

MAYER WISOTSKY

THE WOODCARVER'S SON

The woodcarver's son said to his father
As he looked at a stump
His father brought into the shop;
"What are you going to make out of that?"

"Make out of it?" the woodcarver said,
"I cannot make anything out of it.
It has already been made.
I can only discover and expose it
To the world."

"Can I discover things in the wood
The way you can?" the boy asked.

"Surely you can," said the carver.
"All you need are the proper tools
And the wisdom to know
When you have found it."

The boy thought a moment then said;
"What would happen
If I didn't know when I found it?"

THE LEGEND OF THE TWILIGHT OWLS

"Then you may carve too much and destroy it,"
The carver mused,
"But then you might find something else."

The father knelt down
And looked his son in the eyes
And said with a smile,
"Listen to the wood when you carve.
It will always tell you
The right thing to do."

July 2, 1997

MAYER WISOTSKY

Searching

Search not the Heavens
Where the stars only glitter,
Search not the Earth
Where reality is bitter,
Search in the Self
Where the truth has been buried.

Here you'll find reasons
For the burdens you've carried.
Here you'll find your essence
Gleaming with a faint light,
Striving to tell all the world
Of its Truth,
Trying to tell you
The path to pursue.

Here is where the search commences
Where illusions dissolve and your
Sincerity is tested.
Here is where reason has nothing to hide,
Where the paradox of existence is your only rule,
Where you search for life's meaning
In meaningless discourse
With people who know nothing,
But the reflection of their dreams.

THE LEGEND OF THE TWILIGHT OWLS

The search is your purpose,
Searching for Truth.
Reality unfolding--creating your Soul
Until you transcend your being,
Go beyond your control,
To the next level of existence:
The bittersweet unknown.

April 1999

MAYER WISOTSKY

Analysis Is for Tomorrow

There is no gap in time or space,
No pause to realize what's gone by,
Or what is to come.
All life is seamless,
Without a beginning, without an end.
Even as we think of yesterday,
Today goes fleeting by.
Or as we plan for the future,
The present disappears.
We are all victims of not living
In the only moment that is real,
The one we never understand,
Can never explain,
But is the one that becomes,
The story of our life.

The hardest chore of Life,
Is just to Be.
No thinking about
What to Be, How to Be,
How we want other things to Be,
Just to Be.
To Be in the rapture of the moment,
The exhilaration of the experience,
The now-ness of reality.
Impressions come later,
Analysis is for tomorrow.

November 19, 2002

A Glimpse of Reality

Life has forced my blood to flow,
My brain to think,
My heart to feel.
I think I have control,
But all I really do is hang on,
While Life twists and turns,
Flinging me from side to side,
Now up, now down,
Now good, now bad.
But in between the battering
There is a pause,
A glimpse of truth.
A fleeting view of the beauty
Of existence,
The miraculous sense of creation.
And slowly I begin to create,
With purpose--with design,
With power,
And with love.
Birth began my journey,
But I will create its end.

2004

MAYER WISOTSKY

The Tower

The Tower of Awareness
How it beckons to me, tempting me--taunting me,
Challenging me to climb,
To seek the Truth,
To go beyond my illusions.
But it never reveals the consequences,
The Dark side of this gift.
"The Truth shall set you free from the illusions,"
But it will also set you apart from the believers of the illusions.
Your friends, your family, your culture.
All the things you experienced as reality,
Can no longer be enjoyed or regretted or even felt.
For you are above them all,
You no longer fit--you no longer belong.
You must now be challenged on a new level,
You must be reborn to an alien world,
Grow as a child--learn as a novice--mature to adulthood,
And seek more truth.
The paradox persists, "More Truth--More Ignorance"
The Holy Grail of Truth holds the bitter fluid of separation.

August 28, 2006

THE LEGEND OF THE TWILIGHT OWLS

LOST

I am not lost,
I just don't know where I am going.
I asked all the people I met where they have been,
So that I might go in some direction,
But all I received was the second-hand truth of which way to go,
So, I took a path and headed for a place unknown.
And as I trudged through uncharted roads and unfamiliar places,
I realized that the path had taught me what I had to know.
That the road was what it was all about,
I had arrived at my destination,
Everywhere!

May 28, 2009

MAYER WISOTSKY

It's All About Ours

Walk among the green, green pastures,
Feel the busyness of Life,
Splash about the ocean's shores,
Breathe the essence of creation,
Lie upon the desert sands,
Watch the star-filled night move by,
And realize the vastness of our being,
The minuteness of our seeing.
We live within our shell,
Creating our Heaven--creating our Hell,
Trying to find the things we need,
Things we think will quell our fears,
"It's all about Me," we cry,
As we tread upon another person's dreams.
Walk among the green, green pastures,
Splash about the ocean's shores,
And when you see a star-filled night,
Remember
"It's all about Ours--not Yours."

August 6, 20013

A Speck of Dust.

We are but a speck of dust,
In the vastness of the universe,
but we are special none-the-less.
For we know the significance of our insignificance.
We know how little we truly know.
That knowledge makes us unique.
We can think about the many whirling worlds beyond our realm.
We can envision spinning galaxies cart-wheeling through a universe
That is beyond our understanding.
We can do this while trudging down the path of life,
As if we knew where we were going.
How brave and courageous to face the unknown,
With nothing but our minds to guide the way!
Nothing but our decisions to keep us safe!
Look out, Oh Universe of Much,
This speck of dust is becoming a storm.

April 8, 2014

MAYER WISOTSKY

The Paradox of Symbolic Thinking

The light is a contrast for the dark,
The open for the closed.
Sounds are only meaningful
With silence between them.
Value is judged by the relationship
Of "what is" to "what is not."
Humans know their world
By connections they form.
The world is cruel when there
Are only two choices to be made.
Paradox is paralyzing
When your future is at stake.
Two dimensions are only symbolic:
The real world has four,
Options galore.
Beware of symbols,
The enemy of reality.
Yet they are the pathway to understanding,
The paradox of symbols.

August 2014

THE LEGEND OF THE TWILIGHT OWLS

Gravity

Answers are attracted to questions,
Order to confusion,
Needs to stability and desires to fulfillment--
The world is filled with the laws of gravity--
Constantly seeking equilibrium.
A place of stillness is always under tension,
Balance is the byword,
Each and every day.

September 15, 2015

MAYER WISOTSKY

A Wise Man Came to Tea

Sit with me while I sip my tea, tell me all the wonders I will see,
When I grow up and turn 53.
Tell me where my youth has gone, where it was supposed to lead me?
I thought I had grown up and become an adult,
But all I have done is grown older.
I wasted time--I wasted life,
Nothing would go to where it was bound,
Just round and round then spiraling into the ground--
Never to be seen--never to be found.
Tell me! Tell me! Show me the path; open my eyes to the silliness I've seen,
Guide me to the golden road of accomplishment,
That I may tell my great-grandchildren of the wondrous things I've done,
And why it matters to reach your goal.
The wise man smiled and nodded his head, as he sipped the steaming cup
And asked, "What kind of tea is this?"
"I don't know" I said--"does it really matter?"
The wise man looked me straight in the eye,
"That is where your youth has gone, many years ago,
That is where your non-accomplishments lie,
What matters, what really matters, only matters now."

October 9, 2015

THE LEGEND OF THE TWILIGHT OWLS

Only in Paradox

I wandered for years through bad news and jeers,
Looking for a life I thought should have been.
It didn't happen--it wasn't there.
Disappointment became my greatest fear.
Then one day I met a man,
Whose message was truly profound
 He said,
> "Take your coat off and stay a while.
> Get to know the common folk,
>> (the ones whose names you always forget.)
> Be that World you are looking for.
> Feel everything as deeply as you can.
> Experience everything with a welcoming hand.
> Don't worry about the contradictions,
> For only in Paradox can truth be born."

Suddenly I looked down,
My coat was off and I was warm.

December 18, 2016

MAYER WISOTSKY

Being Born

All things are seen only through my eyes,
My brain, my understanding.
Everything is my world--my universe.
It is all about me.
Other people see things, feel things and understand things, but not like me.
I look to others to see my reflection in their eyes,
Using them as mirrors of me.
Suddenly, I want to know their world, I want to feel their reality.
Unfortunately…
It's a message coming through my reality.
Their lives are always my version of their lives.
So, in the end, it is still only me.
I long to change my place in that objective world,
See the truth from a different perspective,
Feel the world from a different source (that is not me).
I seek connections without understanding,
I desire relationships without interpretations,
I need essence with no past,
Explanations without bias, facts without faith,
Life devoid of context.
I want the impossible in my seemingly possible world;
This is the paradox of being born.

February 13, 2018

12 o'clock

It is 12 o'clock and all is well.
The bad people are dying and going to Hell.
The world is still spinning, but the climate is not right,
And the good people are dying, too.
How sad that happiness is a thing of the past.
If you live long enough you watch all the people depart,
Be they rich or poor, stupid or smart…
So serious a place where there is no love…
Where there is only the rational, the reasonable,
And the logical.
Where are the emotional responses to life?
The gut level feelings of understanding?
Our connections are real--
Our bodies tell us so.
Our emotions flood our minds,
Our rational thoughts disappear.
We are naked in our need for connections,
Overcome by our sense of belonging,
The affirmation of our being alive
In a world vibrating with aliveness,
All things striving for existence,
Striving to Be.

2018

MAYER WISOTSKY

Nothing is Everything

What did I have to go through to be here?
How much did I have to endure?
Did I ever know where I was going?
Or was it just discovery along the way?
(The Way I did not pick, The Way that leads me now.)
Who then laid out my path?
Or should I even ask?
For I am trapped in the Mystery of Time,
Where all beginnings are endings,
And all endings begin,
Where change can only be measured by sameness
And Black exists because of White,
Where nowhere is everywhere
And I am not yet where I belong.

February 12, 2019

The Tao of Now

What does it take to experience the Now?
A mind full of connections,
A body scarred by the past,
A spirit depressed by dark expectations.
These are the things that keep you from the Now.
So you must restructure your Being.
Stop connecting to all the Known.
Just absorb everything as Unknown,
No answers needed.
All the Past is just the history
Of Someone who no longer exists.
And the Future is just a fun-filled carnival ride,
Exciting, but not frightening.
Each moment you are reborn,
No concept of what is to come,
No memory of what has been,
All impressions are being absorbed,
Not recognized.
All sensations are what they are,
With no connections to what has been.
That is the Now

June 2019

MAYER WISOTSKY

Beautiful Life

There is no cold----just the absence of warmth,
There is no darkness----just the absence of light,
There is no loneliness----just the absence of love.
Negativity does not exist----just a lack of the positive.
So how do you see your world?
Either/or--this or that--black or white--up or down,
Yes or no.
A world of only two choices,
Formatory thinking--a dichotomous entrapment.
The world is bigger than all you know,
Than all you can imagine.
But whatever you can imagine,
Give it a try,
Be different in your look at life,
Be unique--be you
And life will always be beautiful.

January 20, 2020

Gift of All Gifts

As thunder and lightning fill my world
I think about the sunshine I used to see,
The blue skies that looked so peaceful,
But it did not change my stormy days.
I could not think reality away.
Where is the sun when you need it?
Where are the peaceful times,
When you are exhausted?
The world is not made for "cry-babies,"
Or "It's-everybody-else's-faulters."
It takes determination to live life,
And strength to make it meaningful.
Honoring one's life force
With the Gift of All Gifts,
Life in the form of Me.
I cannot waste it on frivolous behavior,
I cannot sleep it away or spend it
Playing meaningless games of power,
Or shameless acts of devotees.
Live it with gusto--live it in the present,
Remembering--attitude is everything.

January 26, 2020

MAYER WISOTSKY

The Cycle of Believing

When believing begins, searching ends.
When faith dies, curiosity begins,
And the world is a place for living,
Fascinated by the miracles of Nature's abilities.
Intoxicated by the beauty of it all,
Then comes the question How?
How does it do what it does?
Searching begins.
Then lastly the question of Why appears,
And belief is born all over again.

February 26, 2020

THE LEGEND OF THE TWILIGHT OWLS

A Poem

A poem can be a call for clarity.
A poem can be a cry for help.
It can give you understanding…
It can show you where you've been.
Poems have the magical power
Of being bigger than life,
And the human power
Of letting you feel the world around you.
Be careful when you read a good poem…
It may change your life forever.

March 14, 2021

MAYER WISOTSKY

Taking a Risk

There are times when you are alone,
But not lonely,
When you are your whole world.
And there are times when you are
Surrounded by humanity, by nature,
By the minutiae of living,
When time is scarce,
And you think you hate everyone
For the pressure they bring.
You live in two worlds:
One world fighting to survive,
The other at peace with the Universe,
Remembering from whence you came.
We humans need each other,
Need Nature to feel whole.
But most of all
We need ourselves.
We need to know the real Us.
"Building our ship as we sail it…"
Be careful…Be wise,
But take the risk of being the real you.

April 11, 2020

The Seekers

If you want to find something in life
You must go looking for it.
And when you are looking for it
You will find many other things
You didn't know existed.
Looking is essential to finding.
So when you are not looking,
When you are satisfied with how things are,
You don't see them anymore…
Contentment
Becomes sleeping…
Sleeping begets dreaming…
And fantasies fill our minds.
Living becomes automatic.
Emotions become unreal.
The automatons who run your body
Have no feelings at all.
You must wake up to live life as a seeker
Of the truth of your world.

May 12, 2020

MAYER WISOTSKY

Asking Questions

If the answers to your questions
Don't seem right,
Maybe you are asking the wrong questions.
The world is full of why;
Your mind is full of because.
To know the moment is to live it,
To have been there,
Feeling a sense of existing,
Understanding life is a quest,
Being able to accept it as wisdom.
Life does not wait for you to catch up.
It is always moving,
And you must move with it.
Happy Trails (or Trials as the case may be).

August 20, 2020

THE LEGEND OF THE TWILIGHT OWLS

The Impossible

Hope is for the hopeless ones,
The ones without purpose or will.
Becoming is a matter of desire
And the tenacity to keep trying.
Life is always a lesson of
Trying to get somewhere
Without a map.
So you must not only know
How to read a map…
But how to make one.
How to choose the path…
How to pick a time to move
And how to wait and rest.
Tough decisions without experience…
So if you want to Become,
Get some experience.
Try something impossible.

November 6, 2020

MAYER WISOTSKY

Can You Laugh, Albert?

The happy sounds of laughter
Rising from a joyful life,
Living in each moment
Of your life…
It feels good to be contrary,
To look at the trials and tribulations
With a sense of humor,
Like an outsider watching
A Punch-and-Judy show.
It is all make-believe,
Lives to be laughed at.
Can you still laugh
When it is you on life's stage,
Gasping for breath
With disaster all around you?
Can you still laugh when it's you
Suffering the pain?
Life is a paradox of emotions,
A gift that cannot be returned,
A curse that cannot be given away.
And that Is Funny…At that You Can Laugh…
Because it is all absurd,
Simultaneously all real.

December 12, 2020

All Powerful

Can I welcome in the thoughts of joy,
And make them part of who I am?
Can I feel good about feeling alive
Each day?
Can I see the world as a place of possibilities?
Can I feel life tingling throughout my body?
Yes I can, so can you…
You are all-powerful to create your life
In any way you wish.
The only problem is to know
The end results of all you do,
And be willing to take the risk.
First you must know you,
Then you must know others,
And finally, you must know
How to recognize reality.
Then you can be
Whatever you want to be.

December 24, 2020

About the Poet
A Short Look at a Long Life

FOR SEVENTY YEARS I HAVE BEEN CHASING truth, understanding, and awareness while looking for the reasons for my existence. I have worked in every kind of job from factory worker to hospital executive, from teacher to counselor, from actor and director to writer and musician, from salesman to manager, from bricklayer to woodcarver, from entrepreneur to consultant, from paperboy to selling vacuums. I have joined philosophical groups, political groups, religious groups, the military and was the president of a college faculty union.

My years of living has given me a huge amount of experience to authentically understand the world. Poetry has been my safety valve. It is the way I can express my understanding of reality in an emotional burst of creativity. These poetic flares started as I was emerging from a ending marriage (with two children) and trying to finish my Master's degree. Feeling lonely and unloved, I tried to express my feelings through poetry. I remarried a second time (two more children) and after 13 years got divorced again. At that point I began searching for who I was deep down, my essence. Poetry was the main expression of my search.

On my 45th birthday, I needed the discipline of a determined man, and I decided to become a vegetarian. That decision helped me discover my lifelong philosophy. I wrote the poem "The Vegetarian" about the incident.

For the next year, I scrupulously examined every aspect of my life, and I got my act together. I started my new life, found my soul-mate, married her, and for 42 years have been living, loving, and sparking out poetry to better understand my changing self and our changing world. This is my Truth.

Poetry as a Medium for Creative Expression

STORYTELLERS PAINT PICTURES with words and symbols in order to explain reality.

Before the written word was the universal medium of communication, the spoken word symbolized an emotional understanding of the world. The music of the voice was seen as an expression of the deepest truth. Poetry connected the oral symbols with music, using rhythm, rhyming, and alliteration.

Poetry touches the deepest feelings. It makes the audience/reader part of the presentation and creates a conversation with the poet.

This is my approach to poetry. I don't always rhyme, but I am rhythmic in my style, leaving space for the symbols to have their effect on whoever is listening to or reading the poems.

If you would like to hear/see poems by me in the future, join the:

Weekly Poems Group at
wisewoodcarver@gmail.com

www.ingramcontent.com/pod-product-compliance
Lightning Source LLC
Chambersburg PA
CBHW060525090426
42735CB00011B/2373